Slowly by Slowly
A journey with Christ, the birth of a ministry

By Patrick S Beard

Indigenous Outreach International
Post Office Box 10173
Jackson, Tennessee 38308-01002
(731) 664-9960
www.ioiusa.org

Copyright © 2009 by Patrick S Beard

Slowly by Slowly
by Patrick S Beard

Printed in the United States of America

ISBN 978-1-60791-999-5

All rights reserved solely by the author. The author guarantees all contents are original and do not infringe upon the legal rights of any other person or work. No part of this book may be reproduced in any form without the permission of the author. The views expressed in this book are not necessarily those of the publisher.

Unless otherwise indicated, Bible quotations are taken from The Holy Bible, New King James version. Copyright © 1982 by Thomas Nelson, Inc.

Some names have been changed.

www.xulonpress.com

Slowly by Slowly

A journey with Christ, the birth of a ministry

Contents

1. A Seed Must Die	5
2. Fifty Cents Would Have Saved That Baby	11
3. I want to live in Africa	19
4. Digging up the Devil	31
5. Sure Enough Africa	39
6. Out of Africa	49
7. A New Beginning	63
8. Brain Damage	71
9. Slowly by Slowly an Egg Will Walk	79
10. Two Questions	93

"Slowly by slowly an egg will walk"
  Ethiopian Proverb

Chapter One
A Seed Must Die

Slowly at first, then gaining momentum the Alitalia flight lifted off the runway in Addis Abeba en route to Rome. It was the funeral for the death of a lifelong dream.

I was thirteen when I first knew that I wanted to be a foreign missionary. Now thirty and having lived less than one year in Ethiopia, I was bound for home in defeat with a sick wife and 30 pounds lighter myself.

Just a few weeks earlier, we had seemed to come to grips with the harsh realities of life in Ethiopia. It was much harder than we had expected, and we had expected very harsh conditions. Separation from extended family and friends back home was difficult. Unreliable electric and phone service was annoying. There was a war going on. Although the front lines were miles from our home, the sound of fighter jets overhead brought more anxiety than comfort. Every meal had to be prepared by hand from scratch, and keeping a home clean was practically impossible in either the dry or rainy seasons. Relationships with fellow missionaries could be strained at times. The air seemed to always be filled with the aroma of diesel exhaust, eucalyptus, rot and sewage. The magnitude of poverty and disease was overwhelming with over half of the four million residents of Addis living in shacks made from garbage. Still, Ethiopia was becoming our home, and I no longer wanted to run away.

In an environment so intense, we had developed some deep relationships. Colin and Hazel were British missionaries who had spent most of the past thirty years in Ethiopia, and they were a great comfort to us. They could have commanded a stiff upper lip, but instead they seemed to empathize with our weakness. They, along with an international prayer group, encouraged and prayed for us.

In our first meeting, Hazel served us tea in proper British fashion. Colin took a long sip of his tea, replaced the cup on the saucer and asked with a smile, "So Patrick, you are a short-termer?"

"Yes, sir."

"Well, I'll let you know right out, I don't approve of short-termers."

Less than a year later at our last prayer meeting in Addis I shared that we were about to leave the country for medical treatment. By that time Colin and Hazel had become dear to us, and Colin's response was, "Well, I think that is indeed a shame."

Although we had lived isolated from non-English speaking Ethiopians, we had developed some relationships with the locals. Gezahenge and Asrat, with their daughter Kalkidon, were our first Ethiopian house guests. They had been asked to help us learn Ethiopian customs and the predominant Ethiopian language of Amharic.

Asrat stood smiling at the door of her simple mud home. She spoke no English, but her arms welcomed us. After hugs and kisses we entered the small room where we would have dinner. The walls were covered in old newspaper and Gezahenge's original artwork. A single dim light bulb gave light enough to eat by, candles at the ready for the inevitable power outage.

The aroma of the meal was appetizing. What Ethiopians lack in presentation they more than make up for in spices and flavor. Although they would not normally eat expensive meat, they had prepared a spicy doro wat (chicken stew) for us. Our two young daughters were treated like royalty.

Our home was modest by American standards, three bedrooms and one bath. However, when we visited Gezahenge's family, we ate in one small room of the mud home. They used the other room to sleep in. Even though our living standards were so vastly different, they never acted like we were awful for having so much wealth. They knew that we were the needy ones.

As we got to know more Ethiopians, their faith and joy became evident to us. Despite hard living conditions, they seemed to have more joy than we did. More often than not the poorer the family, the more spiritual wealth they seemed to possess and the more willing to share of their possessions.

One Ethiopian employee took a keen interest in me and my family. Negash would come to my home after business hours and he would compel me to go with him to pray for the sick and demon possessed. He asked me to preach at his church, and he mentored me in hands-on ministry.

I had served on church staff, attended more worship services than I could count, studied the Bible with mentors, but life in Ethiopia had brought me to the conclusion that I was indeed needy. I had it all, but I was poverty stricken.

Just beyond the razor wire topped gates of our Western-style compound there were disciple makers and church planters who were lacking. I never saw one of these saints begging for bread, but I did know indigenous ministers who would say that going unwillingly without food was a time of God-imposed fasting. I knew many that gave their full-time to the ministry of the Gospel, yet they slept on dirt floors of austere mud huts.

I longed to do good to them. They had done so much good to me, but now I was leaving it all behind. I had no idea if I would ever return.

As the airplane gained altitude and Ethiopia grew smaller beneath us, my tears turned from grief and guilt to relief. I had hated living in Ethiopia, but I found no one with whom I could share that information. Every other day had seemed to be filled with nausea, guilt and frustration. I had had my dream, and it had turned into a nightmare. Now the nightmare was over. We would soon be home.

It seems that God often gives a dream, kills it and then gives it real life. My dream of being a vocational missionary was dying, and as that dream went into the ground, it was a seed that would soon sprout.

Chapter Two
Fifty Cents Would Have Saved That Baby

Growing up in a small town in the hill country of Northeast Mississippi in the seventies, I knew surprisingly little of prejudice. The town of less than 3,000 was about 90% white. Most of our granddaddies' granddaddies were born into these Appalachian foothills and had lived their lives on a piece of red clay that was too hard and dry for cotton farming.

Desegregation of the local schools happened eight years before I entered the first grade. It must not have been too exciting in Fulton because I never heard anything about it, nor did I think it strange to have fellow classmates that were not white. As far as I was concerned there was only one race – the human race, but that would change in time.

My great great-great grandfather was one of the exceptions to the rule of antebellum poverty in Itawamba County. He was a land owner of considerable holdings. Not that it ever did me much good, thanks to his service in the war of 1812 and the need to leave Georgia after winning a "duel" that was fought with a plank from his front porch and ended in the death of a neighbor who had insinuated that my forebear was a liar. It seems that this, my only ancestor of means, also owned a few of his fellow men and women of African descent. This was my grandmother's grandfather and the grudge he held from the loss of the Great Struggle, also known as the Civil War, had been passed on to her in part. Grudges die much slower it seems than loud-mouthed neighbors hit in the head with planks.

My best friend and I did not play cowboys and Indians; we played Civil War. Neither of us wanted to be the Yankee, because we all knew that they were the enemy. It did not matter that they actually won the war; they simply weren't from here. Other kids may have played war with green plastic army men, but Julian and I would ignite cherry bombs under blue and gray plastic replicas of our great-great grandfathers. We were too young to know much about politics or the causes and horrors of war; it was just a kid's game and a sublime way to pass the long hot hours of the humid Mississippi summer days.

As a child I never thought much about life outside of that small Mississippi town, or why anyone would ever want to leave it. I just assumed that I, like my father before me and his father before him, would be a business owner and live happily ever after here in the center of the universe.

It was an idealistic childhood with just enough entertainment to keep me occupied and just enough trips to the hospital to keep my mother believing that I must have an overworked Guardian Angel and some great purpose in life.

We had less than a dozen stations on the local cable system until two stations were added that brought the number to twelve. WGN from Chicago and the Turner Network out of Atlanta opened the world to me in those hours after school. Andy Griffith and Gilligan's Island reruns brought to television the best of a charming Southern town and the romance of a castaway island in the South Pacific. The Saturday matinees brought to life the exotic jungles of Africa in the form of black and white Tarzan movies. Sunday evenings when I was too sick to attend evening church services, Mutual of Omaha brought scenes of Marlin Perkins flying safely in a helicopter over the viper-infested jungles and plains of Africa while Jim, escorted by Pygmies and rifle-toting park rangers, would wrestle Nile crocodiles in order to place a homing device around their necks for the next time we get a hankering to catch up with a man-eating monster. My world was expanding and, to quote Tarzan, "Simba! Simba! Tigewa!"

History and faraway places jockeyed for my attention. As I grew older Civil War reenacting became a popular hobby, and I immersed my free time in the study of the War Between the States and the historically accurate portrayal of a Civil War soldier. My sister's creativity and my father's artistic flare led to daydreams of living in Hawaii and becoming a famous artist. I saw no particular reason to think that these ideals were juxtaposed, nor that I could not do anything and everything I set my mind to. Much like changing the channel from Mayberry to Gilligan's Island I could and would do everything I set my heart to thirty minutes at a time.

One fateful day my world was rocked and it would soon be changed forever. My father had returned from leading a mission trip to Honduras. He had no idea when he planned that first trip that his return would be one of the most influential moments of my life. I was almost a teenager and his display of a machete, photos of distant villages with real-life soldiers grabbed my attention. I would go on the next trip come hell or high water. I was not accustomed to taking "no" for an answer. I was the third of four children, and I came out of the womb shining and stealing the show. My older brother got all the whippings, and I got the benefit of older and wiser parents that were getting too tired to say no.

The next year a team was formed from our local Church. First Baptist Church of Fulton had put its toe in the water of missions a year earlier and a fever broke out across the congregation that lasted throughout my high school and college years. Doctors, pharmacists, nurses, preachers and even an IRS tax collector volunteered for the teams. There was more excitement in those days leading up to a team going out than any revival I could remember.

My mother has no memory now of how or why she and my father let me join the team, but I was soon to be on a Sahsa airliner bound for Central America.

Among my growing number of interests and hobbies, I had been influenced by a fellow Mississippian that created a frog and pig and made it big. Jim Henson's Muppets captured my imagination for a time and I was soon using puppetry as a means to gain attention and get laughs. In addition to winning talent contests with puppet performances, someone had figured out that you could attract prospects to preaching services with a little song and dance beforehand. The dancing was all perfectly legal for a puppet of course, I suppose because they have no legs. So it was decided that I would perform puppet skits between sermons for this evangelistic outreach to a remote village in Honduras.

I loved everything about that trip from the very beginning. The meetings that preceded our departure, the application for a passport, the packing of supplies into cardboard boxes and the road trip to New Orleans to catch my first international flight. Each day was filled with new experiences. But, there was one new experience that I was not prepared for -- the reality of extreme poverty.

I don't really remember many details from that first trip, but I do remember how I admired the short little stocky man who had dedicated his life to helping the poor in Honduras. Charlie Herrington had been told by a mission agency that his health was too poor to serve as a missionary. They were correct; he died in Honduras after only a couple of decades or so of service. But in the time that he served, he started a ministry that has outlived him, has done a mountain of good for the people of Honduras and opened the eyes of a thousand people like myself to what God can do through one man who obeys God by simply serving the poor.

Late one afternoon a mother brought a small bundle to the doctors on our team. As they pulled the rags back a malnourished baby was revealed to be clinging to life by a thread. His body was little more than skin loosely attached to bones. As the generator was shut down for the evening, a Coleman lantern was lighted in a small school room that served as a critical care ward. Into the night the doctors and nurses fought to save the baby's life. As the sun rose over the beautiful rustic mountains surrounding the village of Ocatal and its beams peaked into the windows of the makeshift hospital room, the lantern light faded, and so did the infant.

I can remember as clearly now as almost thirty years ago how the mother wept as she wrapped the body of her dead child and prepared to make the long walk home to bury him. And as though etched in stone the words that I overheard spoken by a doctor were chiseled into my heart for all time, "Fifty cents worth of medicine could have saved that baby a week ago." I would never be the same after that moment. I had gone to bed a child with a head full of dreams and ambition. I awoke to my destiny and the belief that my life would be worthless if I did not use it to help people. I refused to see another baby die for lack of medicine or clean water.

Chapter Three
I want to live in Africa

I traveled back to Honduras more times than I kept a record of. Each trip would confirm my "calling to missions," and I would draw up plans for the day that I would become a missionary to Central America. I even made my fiancée take a trip to Honduras, just so she would know what she was getting herself into.

Lana went to Honduras. She experienced the best and worst of mission life that one week had to offer. I promised her my love. I could not promise a porcelain toilet, but she would have my love. Even though a bout of dysentery caused her to question marriage momentarily, she did agree to be my wife.

Before we were married, I made a trip to Brazil. It seemed like a good idea, and like many zealous young Christians, I found my plans confirmed by God in every wisp of wind or scripture passage taken out of context.

Until the trip to Brazil, my ambition had been to help people in some *tangible* way. We didn't really "help" anybody in Brazil. We traveled a lot and saw all the tourist sites. We went door-to-door to evangelize the Catholics and play baseball with the kids in the park. So it was on this journey that a greater reason for traveling was confirmed within me. People need Jesus.

"No Jesus, Know Fear. Know Jesus, No fear!" My life was becoming a series of catch phases and memorized scripture passages to lead someone down the Roman Road to Jesus and away from the Roman church.

"God loves you! Jesus died for you. If you will just accept Him, He will solve all your problems. Is there any reason why you would not be willing to pray this prayer with me and ask Jesus into your heart?"

In Brazil I questioned my calling to Honduras. I was getting a travel lust and I could no longer see myself living in some poverty-stricken village in Honduras for the rest of my life. Devoting myself to the poor and outcast seemed a bit dull. Maybe I could be a traveling itinerant international missionary. I could offer puppets, drama and compassion under the stage lights in the tradition of Charles Finney, who would do "whatever it takes" to bring them down the aisle. My numbers would be huge as I took my dog-and-pony show to the most rural of places on earth with decent hotel rooms. Why I would be a modern day saint, if we Baptists had saints.

I had much too much to learn.

We began attending a Bible study that was taught by an economics professor. His Friday night Bible study was hosted in his home, and his wife would serve us soft drinks and cookies. After some singing of choruses accompanied by guitar, Walton would open his Bible and pick up where he had left off the previous week. It was a revolutionary approach to the Bible — verse-by-verse Bible study.

After the study one evening Walton asked me, "Can you tell me what the Gospel is?"

The question shook me. Of course I knew what the Gospel was. I had served as a Youth Minister in three churches and gone on a dozen or more mission trips. I graduated from Bible college for goodness sakes. "Yes, I can." Surely I can answer this Sunday school teacher's question.

"Ok, what is it?"

"Well, you see... The Bible. Jesus... Right?"

"The Bible what? Jesus, Jesus who?"

It seems that although I was so sure of my

salvation and had even taken people through tracts, the Four Spiritual Laws, evangelism programs and led them in the Sinner's Prayer, I could not answer the simplest question, "What is the Gospel?"

Growing up in the South as a Baptist I thought Church history started in the 1800's and our only "saint" was Lottie Moon, who was born a daughter of a wealthy slave owner and died as a missionary to China by starving herself to death while feeding her neighbors. I knew very little of the years between AD 33 and 1800, much less how we came to be so egocentric in our approach to missions and evangelism.

"Do you find the 'Sinner's prayer' in the Bible?"

"No."

"How do you know that you are saved?"

Well, I thought, because I walked the aisle at church camp and said that prayer and *meant it* with all my heart. But I would be lying through my teeth. I faked those tears back then, and it had plagued me ever since. I really had no assurance of anything concerning God. I was hoping that it would all pan out in the end, and I would have more pluses than minuses at the grand total.

"Seems to me you are counting on a prayer that isn't even in the Bible for your salvation."

Then genially he let me off the hook, "Brother, I think you will find the answer to my question in First Corinthians chapter fifteen."

It was so simple. Christ died according to the Scriptures. He was buried. He was raised on the third day, and He ascended. That is the Gospel. The Good News is that if we believe this Gospel, profess Jesus as LORD and believe that God raised Him from the dead we will be saved. The resurrection is the Good News of the Gospel; it is the hope and future of all who believe.

It struck me that although I would have said that the Bible is the "Word of God," that I knew very little beyond the few verses I had memorized. I had tried to read the Bible many times starting at Genesis, and I almost made it through Numbers once. I had actually read the New Testament, or at least a few of the Gospels and a couple of the smaller books. For all my "love" of the Bible, I didn't know it very well at all. My religion was based on Sunday school quarterlies, what little of the sermons I had listened to, my opinion and old wives tales. I would have argued that the Bible is the "living Word of God," but actually knew very little of the living Word it professes. The Bible had actually become an idol of sorts, something I dared not place anything on top of or show any disrespect to. Mine was a religion of tradition and osmosis. My beliefs had been spoon-fed to me.

I had believed the Gospel. I can't remember

a time when I did not believe that Jesus is the Son of God and that he died, was buried and raised again on the third day. I believed that Jesus ascended to Heaven and will return again, but I could not even begin to answer a simple question about what the Gospel is. I did believe the Bible and in the Word of God it proclaims. My formulas were found lacking. I was saved and will be saved, but I could not begin to explain what that truly means. It was time to wrestle and fight for the faith I proclaimed so readily.

I had been challenged to a deeper walk as a teen-ager, then again in college. Somehow I continued to rely on my own feelings and experiences. I made commitments; I cried real tears; I even signed rededication cards. I tried to be a "good" guy and please God. Still I was lacking any assurance of salvation. The more I tried, the more lost I felt.

I began to study Scripture with men like Walton. I became angry at all the years I had wasted in the world of opinion rather than study of the Scriptures. Although my previous mentors had suggested it, I simply had not read my Bible. My interest in American history was replaced with a hunger to know more about the history of the Church. What knowledge I was gaining was dangerous and promoting me to pride. It was not Walton's fault. It just seems that I skipped over the teaching of Christ that warns against knowledge without love.

Having the Gospel proclaimed so plainly in Corinthians was a revelation for me. Then reading Romans, Hebrews and other New Testament books in their context made the Scriptures come alive, and they brought comfort as I began to realize that salvation is a work of God. Beginning in Genesis Christ was being revealed, and He was always the plan.

I did believe the Gospel, and that faith was a gift from God. This epiphany was like a salvation experience.

Like Abraham, David and the Apostles, I was saved by faith in Christ!

We joined Woodland Baptist Church where Walton taught a Sunday school class. Woodland was a dynamic church that had a local reputation for being different and Spirit-led. It was the kind of church where ministries were birthed and people were being radically saved. The Spirit of God was so evident in those days, and love was abounding. The facilities were paid for and most money was going toward ministry, benevolence and missions.

Out of the blue I was asked if I would like to go on a mission trip to Africa. This same congregation that introduced me to exposition of Scripture from the Sunday school class to the sermons that were preached was now asking me to consider going to Africa. What was up with all these questions?

"No, I don't believe I would *like* to go to Africa."

"Well, it is just that you have such a heart for missions," Jack, the chairman of the missions committee, said.

I had a heart for missions, maybe, but not missions in Africa.

Ethiopia was in the news in those days. People were starving by the millions all because of pride, ignorance and greed. People were being hacked to death in central Africa. My heart went out to the poor, but that is all of me that would go out to Africa. It was the most barbaric place on earth as far as I was concerned, and my plan was to never set foot on the Dark Continent.

Had he been more forceful, I most likely would never have thought about it again. Force and guilt had almost completely lost its power over me. But Jack is so mild-mannered. He wants so desperately to do the right thing that I have never known him to be aggressive.

Maybe God does want me to go to Africa.

No, surely not. I said I would go anywhere but Africa. So why do I feel so completely torn apart inside? Why am I even giving it a second thought?

Just forget it. Let it go. Don't think about it. Ask Lana; she will kill it. Your wife has a good head on her shoulders.

"What do you think, honey? It is crazy, isn't it?"

"I think you should go."

"What?"

"I think you should go."

"No. You're crazy. I'm crazy for even asking"

"Crazy or not, I think you should go."

I actually found myself beginning to be excited about the prospects of heading to my demise. I would be a saint; after all, aren't all martyrs saints? And if I didn't die I would have some really cool stories. Sure I would be leaving a pregnant wife and my three-year-old daughter, but it would be an adventure.

So, there I was getting on a church bus headed for Memphis to catch a flight that would take me halfway across the world and dump me out in *AFRICA*!

I was going to Africa, land of jungles, tsetse flies, river blindness, man-eating lions, pygmies and vipers. I would be tracing the steps of the greats like Henry Stanley and Dr. David Livingstone. I would be a real missionary now.

The problem with my adventure was that our destination was South Africa which is arguably the most prosperous, modern nation on the continent of Africa. We arrived on a South African Airlines 747 in all the comfort that it has to offer. We proceeded with a throng of tourists and business men through the customs and immigration areas. We were collected in a modern van and driven down super motorways past nuclear power plants and checked into a Holiday Inn where I was hit on by a large overweight white homosexual Afrikaner.

Well, this was not what I expected at all really. "I think I'll go get a Coke from the vending machine. Do you guys want anything?"

"No, we're thinking about going to KFC later."

We spent the next week constructing a church building in a rural village. It was surreal to pass through clean modern towns that had chain restaurants and Shell stations, and then depart from the main road to find small collections of mud huts that constituted villages where poor black farmers live much like their ancestors have for thousands of years.

One evening the village chief paid a visit. He was dressed in a London Fog long coat and shorts. He presented us with copies of photos of himself proudly displaying the sign that he had painted which was posted at the village limits and read "Please Don't Shoot the Lions." I got the idea that there were about as many lions in the area as there were headdress and thong-wearing chieftains.

Strangely, I was hooked. This land of paradox and contradiction offered the best of both worlds. Cities and villages were within sight of each other. Mountains and plains contained a wondrous variety of vegetation and wildlife. Everything that I have come to love about Europe is found in South Africa and you can go on a real safari.

I actually woke from a night in a tent to find elephant dung outside the entrance, and spent the evening of the same day eating a steak dinner in a modern city steakhouse with painted wildlife scenes on the wall of the high-rise in which the restaurant was located. I ask you, how cool was that?

I came back from South Africa with a love for Africa and once again my world had expanded beyond my limited ability to see. Africa was not bad. Africa was awesome. Why had I never heard the good about Africa? I not only loved Africa, but all things African. I had become an African-loving American and would promote everything good about our shared cultures.

My vision was destined to die a quick death, but not before my daughter caught it.

Much like the fascination I had with those items and stories from Honduras that my father brought home, that divinely appointed day Anna-Margaret's three-year-old heart was gripped, and she began to pray every night for almost two years, "Father, I want to live in Africa."

Chapter Four
Digging Up the Devil

I was back to the drawing board. I was approaching thirty and a second child had been born. My dream of being a missionary was growing faint, and the needs of my family were putting pressure on me to advance in some kind of career.

It seems that college had prepared me for just about everything in life except reality. I got a piece of paper that testified to my completion of course work, and I came away without any marketable skills.

"Wow, you have a degree in communications. So, what can you do?" was the common question.

Due to my organizational skills I was offered a promotion at the clinic where I worked as a computer technician and became the manager for four of our satellite branches. Getting things organized came natural to me, and I loved the work at first.

Then I learned that trying to manage thirty women is like trying to hold oil in your hand. My former boss in the computer department was a woman. I loved her as a boss and thought she did a great job. If I did my job, she was happy. Managing thirty women, however, was difficult and stressful.

Before long I began to hate my new career. It was the best job I had ever had, but it was not missions and daily management was not my gift. I needed a distraction. I suppose the Devil himself would do fine.

One of the clinics I managed was located in a small town about an hour's drive from Jackson. Our clinic had a bad name there because we had bought out two local practices, and we were seen as the outsiders.

My boss thought that it would be a good move for me to join the local Chamber of Commerce and build some love with local business owners. I thought this would be a great idea and a new experience for me.

The first meeting I attended, I jumped in with both feet. It seemed that there were committee positions that needed to be filled, and I volunteered for the committee that I felt most interested in – tourism. Now I could not think of many reasons any tourist would come to this rural town, but I thought it might be fun to find some reasons and promote them.

The main asset this small community had in its tourism pocket was its proximity to the river and a state park named in honor of Nathan Bedford Forrest.

Forrest was one of the best known Confederate Generals and had actually earned the nickname "Devil Forrest" for his cunning and force. He and a small band of cavalry had once chased a much larger and better armed force of Yankees for miles as they ran in fear from the battle of Brice's Crossroads. He was a Southern gentleman that could fight like the devil.

Forrest was also famous for founding the Order of the Knights of the Klu Klux Klan shortly after the end of the Civil War. According to legend the Klan was originally a social club meant to preserve the ideals of the Confederacy. Their efforts became violent and criminal, and Forrest distanced himself from the Klan. Later in life he actually became a champion of civil rights, although he was never as successful or well-known in this sphere of his existence.

The Devil Forrest was buried in an exclusive cemetery in Memphis. At the time of his interment the cemetery was located in a genteel white community located near large southern homes. As those homes aged the white people fled to the suburbs. Mannerly charm was chopped up and converted to cheap low-income housing. The minority community had become the majority. And the majority now wanted the Devil out of their back yards.

Many Civil War buffs were dismayed at the disrespect that was being paid to Forrest's grave and a variety of opinions had developed as to the solution, none of which was without great controversy.

During a tourism committee meeting, someone suggested that it might be a good idea to dig up Nathan Bedford Forrest and inter him at the state park that bore his name.

"That is a great idea," someone said.

"No, it isn't bad press and all."

"Any press is good press."

"I don't think so."

"Someone needs to head it up."

Vainly I tried to rein in the madness. "Head what up? Hang on a second; let's think about what we are saying here."

"Hey, Patrick aren't you a Civil War buff?

All in favor of Patrick being the committee chairman, say 'Aye'."

They really did hate our clinic.

A few months earlier I had been denied access to a local African Street Festival based on my race. I wanted to publish a magazine about Africa that I hoped would fund my mission endeavors. I was shocked when I was denied access to the festival because I was white, and local media had a heyday with the information that was leaked by a friend. The headlines of the Sunday edition read, "White Vendor barred from Street Festival." I was the White Vendor, but somehow my name remained a mystery through the weeks of media frenzy. I dodged a bullet and my fifteen minutes of fame were anonymous.

Now I am being asked to re-inter the Devil Forrest. So, that's it? After all this time I'm going to die a very public death. I can see it now. Hell's Angels escorting the hearse, state troopers escorting the Hell's Angels, the civil rights leaders celebrating and the KKK protesting. God only knows how much press we would get if it hits the paper about the Anonymous White Vendor being the Very Public Devil Digger Upper. The headlines that were destined to come would be appropriate for a supermarket tabloid. Sure, I want to be sacrificed for corporate gain and those tourism dollars.

"Lord, I want to go! Anywhere! Please

open the door!"

It was Friday the 13th of December when my boss called me into his office.

"Well, we are downsizing the management division of the clinic. We are now only going to have two satellite managers instead of four."

"I see."

"You are not one of the two we will keep."

Relief poured out of me, "Praise the Lord!"

"Excuse me?"

"I said, 'Praise the Lord!' I have been begging God to move me." Besides I don't think anyone but I had the slightest grasp of just how bad it would be to dig up the Devil Forrest.

"Well, I have laid off two other people today and you are the first with that reaction."

"I've been miserable. I hate my job, and I have wanted to be a missionary practically my whole life."

"Well, it seems that God certainly hears your prayers."

For years I had wanted to move overseas. Each opportunity led to disappointment. We did not qualify for service or we were having a baby or fill-in-the-blank. Some reason would come up, and we were just not ready.

As I made my way home from the clinic that day, I pondered how I would tell my dear wife that I had just lost the best job I had ever had. It seemed crazy to say, "I lost my job today. I think it is time to go overseas," but that was the best I could come up with. I figured the dust would settle, and after a few days the shock would wear off. Then I would start a new job somewhere else and continue to be frustrated.

When I arrived home and blurted out my layoff and the fact that I thought it was time to go overseas, my wife replied, "Well, I have been praying that God would show you that. I think so, too."

So there I was almost thirty, and the doors were finally open.

I can see now how God was using all of these events and the vanity of almost a decade of waiting to conform me more to the image of Christ. When I was thirteen, I could not wait to grow up and be a missionary. When I finished college, I could not wait to go overseas as a missionary. For the decade after college, I struggled to find some way of getting overseas as a missionary. Had I known what was coming, I think I would not have been nearly so anxious, but rather taken advantage of these years of discipleship.

It concerns me greatly how zealous young Christians will race to the finish line only to crash and burn. It concerns me even more how often we disobey the Scriptures and put novices in positions of authority only to witness their self-destruction some years later. We protest that even the Apostle Paul instructed Timothy not to allow anyone to "despise his youth," although Timothy was likely at least thirty when Paul wrote that encouragement.

Jesus was approximately 30 when He started His public ministry on Earth. We don't know much about the days between His birth and His first public miracle, other than He grew in wisdom. God incarnate spent 30 years preparing for the most dynamic ministry the world has ever seen. Yet we expect to be leaders in missions at the ripe old age of twenty-one or twenty-five.

Certainly God uses the zeal of youth to advance His Kingdom, but we should never sidetrack our own discipleship in a rush to minister to others. Clouds without rain and empty cisterns can minister to no one.

Chapter Five
Sure Enough Africa

It had been almost two years earlier when my three-year-old daughter began praying on a nightly basis to live in Africa. I thought it was sweet, but Africa was still not on the radar as far as I was concerned.

Being Southern Baptist I knew the only legitimate way to be a missionary was to get a job with the International Mission Board of the Southern Baptist Convention. Charlie, the inspirational missionary from my childhood, had been independent, a "faith" missionary, but even he would have gone SBC if it were not for his health issues. It was a great package that included a nice home, auto, travel, insurance and maybe a house worker or two.

My wife and I attended a candidate conference and we were eventually offered a position with the IMB. We dug through hundreds of requests from around the world as we looked for the perfect fit. So many requests seemed worthy, yet I was not qualified or they did not want a couple with children. I saw the request in Ethiopia and quickly passed it over pretending that I did not see it.

I knew about Ethiopia: famine, war and pestilence on a Biblical scale. A decade earlier we were singing songs about famine and seeing bloated baby bellies attached to walking skeletons on the evening news. Band Aid and Live Aid raised millions of dollars that seemed to only be a drop in the bucket of need. What person in their right mind would go to Ethiopia?

My wife Lana looked long and hard at the job listing in Ethiopia. It had been Ethiopia that first caught her attention during her teenage years. She was being drawn to Africa, and she realized that God had been using the prayers of a child to prepare us. But, Ethiopia wasn't South Africa.

"Photographer needed in London." London! Perfect, especially because it was London, which was about the only place in the world in which I thought Lana would be totally overjoyed to live other than the good ole USA. No famine in London. No war in London. No pestilence on a Biblical scale in London. There would just be lots of rain and friendly Brits with great accents in London. Not the best food in the world, but then France is just a Chunnel ride away. I was to make trips to North Africa and take lots of photos to use in promotion of missions.

Visions of grandeur danced in my head. Go on exotic photo shoots in Casablanca, and return home to my loving wife at our flat in London. Can missions really be this cool?

I left the interview with my number one pick as London and had every reason to believe that it was in the bag. Our second choice was the same job in Bangkok, Thailand, which would have been fine. I had no third choice.

Lana pondered our decision, and she followed my lead. Ethiopia seemed such a stretch for us, and London seemed perfect.

Coming home to Anna-Margaret and explaining to her that we had accepted a job in London was a heart break for her, and I am sure a delight to our parents whose Christmas had been ruined by our announcement that we would be volunteering as missionaries to some God-forsaken part of the world.

"But, London is not in Africa," Anna-Margaret said.

"No, honey, but Daddy will be working in Africa, and maybe you can go with him on one of his trips."

"But I want to live in Africa."

"Maybe you can marry a missionary to Africa when you grow up."

"But I want to live in Africa while I am still a child."

"Well then, you should have said that in your prayers."

That night she began to finish her prayers with, "I want to live in Africa while I am a little child. Amen."

Two weeks later we were notified that our job in London had been cancelled due to a "paradigm shift." I had no idea what a paradigm shift was, and I did not appreciate it shifting my job out of existence. Basically it is a business term that means everything is changing because what we have been doing "isn't working." How could God be leading one way today and take an abrupt about face the next?

"So, I guess we will be going to Thailand."

"Well, not exactly. You see that job was cancelled too. Basically the whole department you would have worked for does not exist anymore."

"So, it's back to the drawing board?"

"Well, actually we have two jobs we want you to consider. One job is in Kazakhstan and the other in Ethiopia."

I knew about Ethiopia. I was not really up to date on my "stans" other than I knew they were part of the Soviet Union until very recently. "Tell me about Kazakhstan."

"Well, it is cold. You will live on the 13th floor of a Soviet-built apartment complex and they don't turn the heat on unless it gets below freezing."

"What do you know about Ethiopia?"

"70 degrees year round, they eat spicy food and drink lots of really strong coffee. As a matter of fact there are some missionaries to Ethiopia visiting in Tennessee right now if you would like to meet them." It is so obvious now that we were setup. God and man conspired to move us toward destiny.

Seventy degrees, spicy food and strong coffee? I thought the Garden of Eden did not exist anymore.

David and Pam were a fascinating couple. They spoke about Ethiopia like it was a lost paradise. It was obvious that they loved Ethiopia and her people. We were completely taken in with their description, and our fears were consoled. In the excitement of the moment, I was taken in. I faintly remember what should have been a sobering statement, but with a huge smile David said, "Look.

I'll be honest. The capital city of Addis Abeba is a sewer, but we love it!"

We were sold. How much of a coincidence could it have been that Anna had been praying to live in Africa? Didn't our hearts burn when we read the job request from Ethiopia? Wasn't Ethiopia the place that Lana as a youth felt drawn to because it had such need? How strange that this couple was visiting Tennessee at the moment we were making a decision about where to go. Too many arrows pointing in the same direction and it becomes obvious which way to go.

"Ethiopia? Is that in Africa?" Anna asked.

"Definitely honey. You don't get any more Africa than Ethiopia. It is sure enough Africa."

For the months of preparation that lay ahead, there was the joy of an answered prayer, and the anticipation of a life-long dream that was about to come true, and not just my dream, but the dreams of my wife and daughter as well.

I was excited. I was almost thirty when we got our assignment as real life missionaries. I knew when I was thirteen that I wanted to be a missionary. Now I was about to actually do the thing that I had always wanted to do with my life.

It was such a blast to sell most of our worldly belongings and make the preparation to leave the failures of the past behind us. I had enjoyed my life up to this point, but now I was finally getting to do that thing that had been in my heart for so long.

We spent the better part of 24 hours traveling. A stopover in Germany was just over half-way, and we were exhausted when we got on the flight to Addis. Still our anticipation grew as we crossed over the Mediterranean Sea and the mouth of the Nile. Exotic ancient lands stretched beneath us and the distance from home seemed very great.

Our arrival at Bole International Airport was on a rainy night. The old airport was everything one would expect in a third world country. Soldiers in tattered uniforms carried AK47 machine guns. Grime was worn deep into the cracks of the stone floor. A sign that hung crooked directed passengers to the baggage area where a broken down carousel struggled to distribute the luggage. It was an ominous place that reeked of years of neglect and mismanagement.

Once we were through customs and immigration with our kids and earthly possessions in tow, we crossed the barriers to be greeted by a small group of very excited missionaries.

As we got into the van, Lana asked, "Where are the seat belts?"

"There are a few cars here with seatbelts, but you will not need them here. You can't really drive that fast in Addis." Regardless, Lana found a seat belt and strapped Joy into it.

Within a few moments we were slowly making our way down the streets of Addis, dodging what potholes we could, bouncing in and out of others.

Not far down the road we saw donkeys and sheep walking the city streets. Beggars were Dumpster diving for fresh garbage. Buildings were darkened as the power was out in many parts of the city. Shadows of armed men guarded everything that had any value.

"So it looks like there is a lot of crime?"

"No, not really. Not much violence anyway. Even with the war and all, it is really safe here in Addis."

"War?"

"Eritrea. But since the Soviet Union fell apart, Eritrea doesn't have a fresh supply of bullets. They even started throwing rocks at each other on the border. Nothing to worry about really."

Nothing to worry about. Really?

We continued down the pothole-ridden streets and the van was engulfed in a huge sinkhole. Sparks flew from the bumper as it scraped the pavement. Everyone in the van was airborne for a second.

No need for seatbelts. Really?

We left the "good" road and continued down a gravel road. From the gravel road, we turned onto a dirt road, and past a refugee camp where 7,000 homeless people had lived in tents that were rotting. Turning off the dirt road onto a side street, we finally arrived at a ten-foot high gate of a compound that was surrounded by a high fence topped off with razor wire. Another machine gun-bearing guard unlocked the gate and saluted us as we drove in.

"We have put some food in your pantry, and there is some filtered water. Just don't drink the tap water. We will be back in the morning once you have had time to rest. We are so glad you're here. Bye!" With that, the entourage left us to our new home.

"What have I done?" I thought. " I want to go home."

Chapter Six
Out of Africa

Our first full day in Ethiopia we awoke to the early morning chants of an Orthodox priest being broadcast from the tower of a nearby church. I walked into the yard and was greeted by the guard who turned out to be a very grandfatherly man who, much like Deputy Barney Fife of Mayberry, actually owned no bullets. There was such a wondrous variety of birds and flowers in our yard that I could not wait to wake my sleeping family to see the beauty of our new home.

In time Ethiopia did become our home. I would be lying to say that I loved Ethiopia, but it felt like a familiar place. Addis was becoming home. The streets I traveled freely, and the shops I frequented. I even came to expect to see the mentally ill naked guy that generally had a rock in his hand in his regular territory near Mexico circle. I knew where to watch for potholes. I knew where to get a good pizza. I knew to expect inefficiency in government offices. At times maddening, at times wondrous, but always strangely familiar.

My job with the Baptist Mission was one that was familiar in many ways as I was the Media Center Manager. Print media was our main production, and I had lots of experience. Later we worked on a storying project to broadcast the stories of the Bible from Genesis to the Great Commission on radio and audiotape.

It was during the production of the Bible stories that I got to know Negash Gemeda. Negash had worked for the Baptist Mission since the famine times in the early eighties. He was only ten years older than I, but he had a depth about his spirituality that I admired. Negash seemed to be content with his job, but he was always looking for ways to minister to the people directly.

Negash's father had taken a job as a gardener with an early Baptist missionary forty years before my arrival in Ethiopia. Negash was just a boy when John Chang shared the Gospel with him and gave him a New Testament in his language of Amharic. It was this encounter that Negash pointed to as the beginning of his conversion.

His salvation was radical and his commitment was deep. This pilgrim would progress through the valley of death on his way to a deep relationship with Christ. Negash, along with many missionaries, saw the faces of death as thousands starved. Grain was delivered by the ton, but life seemed to be meaningless in this macabre parade of humanitarian aid. Emaciated bodies were strewn across the desert and money was pouring in from the West. Missionaries proved to be all too human and cynicism was ordinary in the intense work environment. Yet a strong sense of life and death gripped him, and he witnessed the joy of salvation in the valley of death. Negash, although he had his struggles, became a devout and powerful evangelist. His fear died on the desert as he experienced God's forgiveness and the urgency of sharing the old, old story to dying men.

Walking to work when he could have easily afforded to take public transportation, Negash would pass through one of the worst neighborhoods in Addis. He purposefully built relationships with the children who lived at the garbage dump so that he might persuade some to come home with him and change their lives. One of those young men now serves as a worship leader in Ethiopia and has written a beautiful song about God lifting him from the garbage heap and setting his feet on a high place.

Sitting in an office was not exactly my dream come true, nor was it Negash's preferred way of spending his days. I wanted to be a missionary and that desire was planted by seeing tangible love displayed to the poor. Negash sensed my angst and he pursued me after hours. He would take me to pray for the sick and demon possessed. He taught me the joy of simple obedience.

I had been taught not to give to beggars.

"When we give to beggars we cause a dependency problem and furthermore they will most likely misuse the money for some sinful purpose." Yet, my conscience would plague me each time I would say to a beggar, "Xavier Yestalin" (May God give to you on my behalf.). I noticed that Negash would give to beggars, especially the lame and mothers with children.

"I've been told not to do that, but I feel guilty when I don't give."

Like a kind father, Negash asked me, "What does Jesus say?"

"Jesus said to give to those who ask, but I cannot give to every beggar in Addis."

"What are they asking you for?"

"Some ask for money; some ask for bread."

"Exactly, they are asking you for enough money to buy a piece of bread. That would be 20 Ethiopian centime, or about 2 and a half pennies of your money. Couldn't you give 2 and a half pennies to a beggar in Jesus' name?"

It was so simple, yet so profound. What did Jesus say? I had it in my ability to bless someone in the name of Jesus.

On my next trip to town, I took my daughter

Anna-Margaret with me, and we stopped at a bakery to purchase a bag of bread. As we would stop at an intersection and beggars' hands would fill the open windows of our van, we would listen to hear what the beggars were asking for. If they said "centime" we would give change; if the request was for "dabo" we would hand them a piece of bread.

As my daughter placed a piece of bread in the hand of a leper "ba Yesus sim" (in Jesus name), the beggar replied to her, "Xavier Yestalin." (May God give to you on my behalf.)

I had been so busy learning how to be a missionary that I had forgotten that Jesus is the Word. He spoke the very words of God and those words were meant to be taken literally. I was looking for the deeper meaning behind the words of Jesus, and trying to figure out what He "really meant." In the process, I had become the Pharisee who would "bless" with empty words when it was in my ability to actually and tangibly bless someone.

Anna-Margaret had prayed to live in Africa. When my wife became pregnant, she began praying for twins. Somehow this child was very in tune with the will of God.

When we had the first ultrasound, Anna-Margaret was with us. We asked the technician if

there was just one baby. He said, "Yes, just one."
A few minutes later, when we asked again if he was sure there was only one baby, he laughed and asked, "Is this a serious question?" I told him about Anna-Margaret's prayers, so he looked once again. "Oh my goodness! There are two babies! Look! Two heads, two bodies, two babies!" Shocked, he looked at Anna-Margaret and said, "Would you pray for me?"

One day Negash asked me if I would be willing to meet a young mother and her dying child.

"I could pay for her to take her child to the doctor."

"I've already done that, but the doctors say there is no hope."

"Well, then I don't know what I can do. There is no hope."

"There is always hope, brother."

I had witnessed the death of a child in Honduras, and I vowed to never do that again.

Gannett was a young mother and her husband had abandoned her when it became obvious that their son Micah was failing to thrive. Most likely in his shame of not being able to provide for his family in an economy with 45% unemployment, he transferred the guilt to his wife and walked out the door. Gannett's family was poor and they could do very little to aid her. The Orthodox church she belonged to was doing its best to minister to masses of poor, and her priest was little help. Gannett was culturally Orthodox and rarely attended worship, but she had not heard the Gospel as her congregation had services in the ancient liturgical language of Geez.

Gannett lived on 2 dollars per month that she made as a water bearer. She would walk to a stream, fill a large jug with water and sell the water in her neighborhood. Her rent took half her income, which left her about one dollar a month to purchase food with. Not only was her child dying, Gannett was starving as well.

Negash had spotted Gannett on the road and he could see the poverty of spirit in her frightened eyes. Her child was dying and she was helpless. She had no faith; she had no hope; and she had no love.

There was a knock at my door and when I opened it, there stood Negash, with Gannett and her baby swaddled in rags.

"I think this is ok with you?" Negash asked with a smile.

I invited them in, and Gannett unwrapped

the skeletal body of her two-year-old son Micah. His weight was about eight pounds, which is the birth weight of many American children.

Micah gasped for each breath and the wheezing proved he was clinging to life. His eyes were rolled up revealing a sick yellow color. Puss drained from his ears. He was barely alive.

"What do you think we should do?" Negash had just brought a dying child to my home, and he had the audacity to ask me what to do.

I mumbled in reply, "I think we should pray?"

"That is a great idea, brother!" was Negash's enthusiastic reply.

I knew that Gannett was not a Christian. What faith she had was lost because of the unloving, fatalistic attitude she had experienced from her Orthodox congregation. Furthermore, she would have little to no reason to believe in Jesus if our prayers were not answered.

In the most pathetic prayer I have ever uttered, we laid hands on the mother and child.

"Father, we are about to ask for a miracle, and this lady does not believe in you. I don't really know if you are going to answer, but we believe that you can. If you don't, this lady will not believe in you, so please, in the name of Jesus, heal this baby."

Micah was healed.

Within a month Micah had doubled his weight and his eyes were now bright and full of life. Gannett brought Micah to our home where we took pictures and weighed him. Far from wheezing, he was now screaming as the tall white missionary took him from his mother's arms to put him on the scales. It was a wonderful day of rejoicing.

One week later I was awakened by an early morning phone call from Negash. "Brother I have some sad news. Micah died last night."

I was in shock. "But God healed Micah."

"Yes, brother, God did heal Micah, but he got pneumonia a couple of days ago, and he was still weak from malnutrition."

"Why didn't Gannett call?"

"She does not have a phone, and besides she said that you have already done too much."

"But, Negash, fifty cents…." There it was again. Fifty cents worth of medicine would have saved a life. This time I was there, but it still happened. I did not understand, and I was angry at God.

We purchased a simple casket and took it to Gannett's home, which was a two-room shack—one room for the people, the other for the animals. Everything she owned was in a neat pile in the corner. A change of clothes, a few plastic containers, a simple coal stove for cooking, a few odd items and a plastic mattress stuffed with hay lay on the floor.

The lawn was filled with neighbors from various evangelical churches. They had heard about the death, and they had come to help as they could. Someone had made coffee. Someone else had provided a grave in a cemetery across town.

I sat in my van watching the men prepare the casket. Why would God heal a child only to have the child die a few weeks later? Why did Micah's mother not call me when he needed only a few pennies worth of medicine? Did God heal Micah to begin with?

Some twenty or more people, along with the tiny casket packed into my 13 passenger van. My frustration only grew as we wormed through the traffic, animals and people that packed the pothole filled streets.

At the cemetery the men dug a hole just large enough for the tiny casket grave between two graves. People crowded around. I kept my distance.

One of the church elders came to me and asked if I understood what Gannett was saying as she beat her chest in mourning. My Amharic was limited to only a few meager expressions at best, and I had no idea what she was saying. This dear brother began to translate.

"Why Micah? Why? Why did you die now? Why did you not die a year ago when no one cared about you? Look, Micah! Look! Your fathers and your mothers are here. Your new family-- they are here. I will miss you, Micah. But I know that I will see you again. I will see you again."

At that moment I looked around, and I saw this great cloud of witnesses, our brothers and our sisters in Christ. People from different congregations had come together to love this poor single mom as she grieved for her dead child. Before us stood our new sister, who only a few weeks before had no faith, no hope and no love. Today she stood before us as a woman of faith, filled with hope and surrounded by the love of God.

On the way home from the funeral Negash began to weep. "You are leaving, brother."

"Yes, but I will be back. We are only going to Europe to have the babies, but we will be back."

"No brother. You are not coming back. It will not be that way. It will be good, but it will not be that way. God is going to do something that we don't expect."

Not long after that strange conversation, we were in a crisis. Lana had become very sick with a bacterial infection in her gut, and our Ethiopian doctor insisted that we leave the country for medical care. Lana was in the second trimester of pregnancy and, with a miscarriage threatening, we needed to leave Ethiopia within the week or our doctor would not sign permission to fly.

I emailed my counselors back home and asked for advice. One reply came from Walton, my long time friend and mentor. He simply said, "Love your wife as Christ loves the Church and gave Himself for her."

But what about the Scripture that teaches I should love God more than I love my wife? Am I not denying God if we leave the country? What about faith? If I have enough faith, won't God heal her?

Missions had become an idol to me. It was my way of "being God." I had the power to change people's lives and make a difference. It was an intoxicating idea, but wicked to the core.

It was not a desire to see God glorified, nor was it to simply obey His commands that had first led me to the mission field. It was a desire to do something big for God and myself. Even my desire to see God glorified can be the most egotistic thing I could do. How can a man add to God's glory? How can a man "do" anything for the Creator of the universe? The whole idea is a mix of the sublime and the ridiculous. Somehow I had come to believe that I had it in my power to add to the greatness of God. My misguided belief seemed to give me power over God.

I felt that going home would be failure, and somehow displeasing to God. My interpretation of Scripture had perverted my view of God into some kind of sadistic egocentric maniac that played with our lives like a man would play chess. But I was beginning to see that God really does love us. His love is real and tangible. Loving my wife and denying my vocation was the most godly thing I could do. I would be proving my love for God by loving my wife and caring for her needs. What better display of God's love toward us than to deny ourselves in favor of those in need? Doing all that we do "to the glory of God" does not add to His glory.

God was not concerned about what I could do for Him. I believe His concern was that I simply obey His Word. God does not require sacrifice, but obedience. God desires that His love be manifest in us and through us. His love is not selfish nor is it self-serving. His love is not conceited. His love is patient, kind and enduring.

Within a few days, we were on the only four seats available on the Friday flight out of Addis Abeba. The future was uncertain, and I was sad to leave my new friends behind, but I knew that I had made the right decision and that our future was in the hands of a loving God. Lana's sickness was a curveball for us, but it was God's way of moving me from a faith of my own choosing to a faith of simply following.

Chapter Seven
A New Beginning

We arrived in Memphis exhausted, weak and sick. Lana was collected from the plane in a wheelchair. When my mother saw how gaunt we looked she began to weep.

America now seemed foreign to us. The children marveled that they could drink tap water. McDonald's tasted like a gourmet meal. People were in a hurry, and few listened long enough to hear much of our experience in Ethiopia. Culture shock began to set in immediately.

We had sold or given away most of our possessions before we moved to Ethiopia. We were home, but we were living in a borrowed house, getting medical care from sympathetic Christian doctors. I looked, but could not find a job.

My plan was to return to the mission field as soon as possible. The twins would be born; we would get everyone healthy, and we would leave. I disliked the decadent consumer-driven, task-oriented society of America now. I was also beginning to hate the Church in America. How could there be so much indifference to a suffering world? How could American's justify spending so much money and time entertaining themselves?

We made the mistake of going out to eat at an all-you-can eat buffet. A table was surrounded by overweight pastors who were joking about how much they had eaten. Bones and scraps piled high as one of the plump shepherds returned from the dessert bar with a small mountain of sweets. "There ain't much left brothers!" he boasted of his plunder.

I wanted to turn their table over and begin beating them with a whip. How could they boast of gluttony? They were no better than the drunkards they routinely damned to Hell. I knew ministers in Ethiopia who would not eat as much in a month as this assembly had consumed in one gastronomical orgy.

Everywhere I turned I saw a wealthy church that was spiritually poor, blind miserable and naked. Evangelical congregations seemed to be trying to outdo each other with their entertainment complexes. Many local churches were spending more on interest payments than missions, in a vain effort to "minister" to people.

Having just returned from a nation where people starve to death and twenty dollars could literally change someone's life, it was easy to see the error of our ways. Few seemed to understand the rage that was boiling below the surface. God was being very patient with me, but a hard lesson was only a few months away.

My longing to return to the mission field was beginning to morph into a new vision. So much of my time in Ethiopia was spent just trying to survive. I believed that my vocation was to "make disciples," but I seemed to be unable to accomplish this task in a nation that was not my home. Other foreigners had been able to accomplish this task, but they were apparently of heartier stock and had sacrificed at least a decade of their lives before seeing much true fruit.

I knew Ethiopians who were gifted ministers, and I knew Negash was a disciple maker because he had discipled me. Many of these native disciple makers were in great need. These were righteous men who would declare a fast when they had no food in the pantry rather than go to the streets to beg.

I had had no success in finding gainful employment. We continued to live in borrowed homes, and every opportunity seemed to slam shut in my face. It was at this lowest point in my life that a revelation would come.

Although I had not been able to get a job, we had money when we needed it. God had provided homes, vehicles, food, clothing and even medical care. We had want of nothing. At times God would provide an odd job for pay, other times groceries would be delivered by fellow church members. There were so many miracles of provision in those days that it was like an adventure to see how our needs would be met.

I was the son of a "self-made" man, and I had earned a regular income since I was fifteen. The sad reality was that I was of very little use to God, if any. It was humbling to be the recipient of so much charity. I had gone from "thinking God sized" to not even being able to feed my family. I was coming to the end of myself, and I stretched out in the floor and begged God to kill me or tell me clearly what to do.

In these dark days of self-loathing, I read the book of First John. "If you see your brother in need and don't have compassion on him, you don't love God."

I was a brother in need, and many American Christians were proving their love for God by loving my family in tangible ways. We have brothers and sisters in Ethiopia that are in great need, and our love for God could be proven by being generous to them.

I wondered if it was possible that God might

allow and empower me to do one simple thing in obedience to His word – have compassion on my poor brothers in Ethiopia. The idea quickly developed in my mind, and I shared it with my mentors.

"Let's see, a homeless, unemployed man wants to start a ministry that provides a regular income for poor Ethiopian ministers? It must be a God thing!"

I received encouragement from my pastor and many who knew me well. Even my dreams were vivid and encouraging. Not everyone was enthusiastic, and some were very negative, but I could not stop thinking about this unique and simple ministry.

We met at Walton's house, where I shared the idea with a group of five men. Questions were raised and answered. We prayed for awhile and then drew up papers that expressed our plan to begin Indigenous Outreach International on January 1, 1999. Our hope was to support five Ethiopian ministers within six months. The support would be fifty dollars per month, given as a love gift, and sent by Western Union. The idea was simple and we had five foundational pillars to build upon: faith, discipleship, edification, authority and love.

Indigenous Outreach would be a ministry that was begun and operated by faith, and promotes faith in Jesus Christ. We would be purposeful in the making of disciples both at home and abroad. We would function for the edification of the Church through the exercise and promotion of spiritual gifts such as teaching, giving and service. We would support local authorities and look to local leaders for direction in ministry. Most of all we wanted to display the love of God in tangible ways by helping to meet daily needs of poor ministers, orphans and widows.

Within four weeks of the meeting I received a first class ticket to Germany that had been donated and support for five Ethiopian ministers. Still I needed $672 for the ticket from Germany to Ethiopia, and the exact amount came in two checks on the same day – they had both been mailed the day before I even knew the amount to pray for.

I had never flown in First Class until I was homeless and unemployed.

"So what do you do?" I asked the man seated next to me.

"I'm a Mercedes dealer. And you?"

"Oh, I'm homeless and unemployed, but I'm on my way to Ethiopia to start an organization to support poor ministers."

A NEW BEGINNING

I met with Negash and shared with him the desire to support indigenous ministers in Ethiopia. Furthermore, I wanted him to be the coordinator for the ministry in Ethiopia as he would know better than I the local authorities and the ministry.

"Negash, I want you to be the first missionary we support."

"Well brother, I think this must be from God. I am honored to serve as the coordinator, and I do know many ministers who are in need. But I will do this as a volunteer; there are others who have greater need than I do."

The five men that were selected had each been in full-time ministry, but none were receiving enough to meet their needs. We gathered in a borrowed room, and I told them of the plan to give them each fifty dollars per month.

"Yes, that is beautiful, but what do you want?" they asked me.

"I just want to bless you."

"Yes, yes. Praise God. But what do you want?"

"God said that we are to be generous and to especially honor those who devote themselves to teaching and preaching. So I just want to obey Him."

For the third time the question came, "But, brother, what do *you* want?"

It was unbelievable to this tattered assembly that anyone from the West would simply give them a regular income with no strings attached. No program to develop, no agenda, no sales pitch, just a simple gift of love.

"Look, you are my brothers in Christ, and I know that you are in need. I want to prove my love for God by loving you in deed and truth. What do I want? I want to obey God and love you."

As the message sank in, two of the ministers explained that they and two other ministers had agreed to share their income.

"Fifty dollars each is a lot of money. Can we share it with two more missionaries?"

I began to weep.

We had asked God to give us five missionaries to support, but now we would be supporting seven with only $250 per month.

Chapter Eight
Brain Damage

When I returned to America I was eager to share about my time in Ethiopia, the amazing story of how Negash refused money, and how two would be sharing their meager income with two others. In many ways it was a confirmation of the fledgling ministry. However, it also made my anger at our greed and waste more profound.

Within a few months of my return from Ethiopia, it became evident that one of the twins was having difficulty. Lauren was not sitting up or developing in the way Kristin was. The doctor reassured us that it might be because she was born small and slightly early. She called it "developmental delay" and said surely Lauren would catch up to Kristin in time.

Lauren started going to therapy, and we continued to hope she would catch up. Days turned to weeks, weeks to months. It was becoming obvious that Lauren was not catching up.

"So, why is she having trouble?" I enquired with a therapist about Lauren's condition.

"She has brain damage. It is serious, and she most likely will need special care for a long time."

Brain damage. Brain damage. Brain damage. It echoed in my mind like a tune that was stuck on a turn-table. I could not think; I could not respond. Brain damage. It is every parent's nightmare and now it was reality. Brain damage. What would this mean for Lauren? Brain damage. What does it mean for us as a family?

I retreated to the prayer chapel at our church and locked the door behind me. I fell onto the prayer bench and cried for hours never making a sentence of more than two words. "Oh, Jesus, oh, Jesus" was interjected into my sobs and dry heaves. I wailed until I had no tears left.

The sounds of my moaning gradually faded, and I was left in the stillness and quiet of a silent God. I was so hungry to hear Him speak that a simple word would have been sufficient. Was God even there? Did He care? Why would He not speak?

Then a shocking question, "Are you angry at Lauren?"

The thought sobered me up immediately.

"Am I angry at Lauren?"

"Do you hate Lauren?"

"No! I think I hate You now! You made her! You formed her in the womb! I believe You are sovereign! I believe You made everything! You made her this way! Why would I be angry at Lauren?!? Why would I hate her?!?"

The bitter thought came like cold water to my face, "Then why do you hate my Church? You say you love me, but you hate your wealthy brothers. You are a liar."

If the Church in America is poor, blind, miserable and naked, why did I hate her? I love the poor, blind and miserable people of Ethiopia. I was actually helping to feed, shelter and clothe some of these poor brothers and sisters. Yet, in my heart I was angry with wealthy American Christians who were no more capable of following Christ than I was. The reality became clear that I was poor, blind, miserable and naked.

My anger at the Church in America only served to prove that I was poverty stricken. My inward condemnations, and sometimes verbal assaults, directed toward those that I considered weak would serve only to condemn me. My lack of discernment was evident.

The fact is there is no American Church.

There is no Ethiopian Church. There is only the Church, the Body of Christ. I could no more choose to love only a part than we should support only a part. We have an abundance of money which is what our brothers in Ethiopia need. Our brothers in Ethiopia have an abundance of faith and joy which is what we need.

The truth is that the supporters and I needed Indigenous Outreach as much as the ministers we would support. God has a passion for His bride, and His love is to be manifest in our tangible displays of love toward His Bride. Secular man can give to a charity, but only God can give charity to a man. The world can feed the hungry, but only the Church can truly love the hungry.

This little girl with no ability to walk, talk or care for herself would become a daily reminder of God's gracious gift of salvation and His mercy. Without speaking a word, she has taught many the simple faith, obedience and unconditional love required of those who would follow Christ.

God had taken me into His arms and fed me Christ. I am a man in debt.

After a couple of years the ministry grew to include thirteen ministers in Ethiopia. It was time to share the ministry with others, and a small team was formed for the purpose of going to see.

With one objective Ross and Ben traveled to Ethiopia. They were to bear witness to the mighty works of God, and report back to the church what they had seen and heard.

As we traveled from the airport to the hotel the two novices huddled for safety. Gun-bearing guards opened the huge gates. Bats flew around the reception desk that was lit with a single candle. Already the team was impressed, and we hunkered down in the hotel room for prayer.

Each day we visited with churches and families that had benefited from the generous support from America. Each story was validated by the meager surroundings.

As the team prepared to leave town, we drove past a home where a wedding feast was being celebrated. Outside the gate was a motley crew of beggars, lepers, blind and lame who were hoping to get the leftovers.

We were reminded of the great feast that is being prepared for those who believe the Gospel. There are those who have been captured by the cares and riches of the world who will not inherit the feast. There are the needy, the poor, the blind, the miserable and naked gathered in the alleys, highways and byways who are being invited, and they will one day feast as never before.

We have been invited to that feast. We have

been compelled to come and feast on Christ, repent and believe. What is our response to such a great love? It must be to love God with all our might and our neighbor as ourselves. Our love must not be in word only, but in deed and truth.

The economy of the world has recently been shaken, and many Christians have watched their life savings vanish in a moment. How much better it would have been to have invested in the Kingdom of God rather than Wall Street, or Main Street. How much better it would have been to give to those who were in need.

The mantle is passing. To be an American today is not the carte blanche it once was concerning international travel. White Westerners have had the stage for the past few centuries in Christian missions, but now the time has come to uphold our brothers and sisters from the developing world as God raises up an army in a valley of dry bones.

In the November 2008 issue of Tabletalk magazine R.C. Sproul said, "It would be no surprise to me if we, in a very short time, will be looking to Africa, to eastern Europe, to Asia, and to Latin America to discover the real power of the Christian gospel."

The Gospel is indeed going forth with

power, and we have a great opportunity unlike any other time in history to see a great expansion of the Kingdom of God. Centuries of missionary zeal have seen the establishment of mission stations in every nation in the world. Great men of God have paid a heavy price as they left their homeland and forged new territory. God is not finished with the Church in the west. God has blessed us beyond measure. We still have a part to play, and we should now be an example of generosity as we once were of evangelical missionary zeal and boldness. We should gladly take up the cross of supporting our poor brothers who are on the cutting edge of frontier missions among their own nations.

Chapter Nine
Slowly by Slowly an Egg
will Walk

Missionaries were added one at a time over the past decade. Partnerships with childcare projects were added to the ministries supported through Indigenous Outreach. Connections in and travel to Ethiopia led to partnerships in Germany, India, Brazil and the United Kingdom. Slowly the ministry expanded.

In the early days some well-intended, and some maybe not so well-intended detractors had raised serious issues concerning the support of indigenous ministers in a third world country. I was surprised to find that there were already about one hundred known ministries supporting indigenous ministers, and there was already missiological scholarship that condemned the practice as "sin against the poor."

The intention in starting this new ministry was simple – obey Scripture by having compassion on my poor brothers. The mission was clear – to make disciples for Christ. The method was elementary - send financial, educational, technical and prayer support. The other major component besides love was trust.

I heard no complaints about Americans or Brits supporting American or British missionaries. Only complaints when the support was going to extremely poor dark-skinned missionaries.

Some who opposed the ministry said that their concern was the corruption of the poor through financial support. However, when the same standard was applied to the support of our pastor I would be rebuked with Scripture that we should honor those who devote themselves to the ministry of preaching and teaching. The irony is that the majority of the ministers supported through Indigenous Outreach are preachers and teachers. The Ethiopians are just as much "our" preachers and teachers as the white Westerners we provide salaries for.

One very logical objection to sending support to the developing world is that money from the West will cause the local congregations in Africa to become dependant on the money, and lazy in giving. "Why should I give if someone else is paying the bill?" However, in the majority of churches that Indigenous Outreach has served over the past decade the support from America has been the catalyst to promote local giving as never before.

In some congregations the money has been matched dollar for dollar, if not more. Furthermore, we are dependant on each other; Christianity is not a faith that is exercised in a vacuum. There are no "self-made" Christians.

The final protest of detractors concerns the authority of the local church. If the money is coming from outside, then someone from the outside is the boss. "We all know that the person who signs the check is the one that controls us." The fear is that somehow Indigenous Outreach would in actuality be controlling congregations in Ethiopia rather than the local believers. But is this true for Americans? If it is true then Jesus fails to be the Lord of most believers in America. Instead our allegiance is to some secular corporation or business. The proposition is ridiculous because Christians should know that God is our provider even when His name is not on the check. Jesus is Lord, and it is His Church not mine, nor the leadership, local or otherwise.

Each of the objections that have been offered over the years has a simple Biblical response. So often we look for some deeper motive in the words of Christ, when all the while He means exactly what He said. "Be generous. Give to the poor. Love your enemies. Do good to them who spitefully use you. If someone commands you to go one mile, go two." There is no ulterior motive, no grand scheme. So often it is not the evangelism of the world that is at issue, rather the issue is personal and individual. The option is simply to obey or disobey. Will you obey Jesus?

The Church in Ethiopia is the Bride of Christ as much as the Church in America is the Bride of Christ. We all share in one body and one blood. The missionaries of Ethiopia are OUR missionaries. We are one family, separated by national boundaries that were established by men.

While great care and forethought should go into the development and implementation of any ministry, objections should not be insurmountable boundaries to obedience. The fact that some people commit adultery should not deter young people from seeking to have a Godly marriage. The fact that planes sometimes crash should not prevent a traveler from flying. The fact that some ministers fall into grievous sin should not prevent the young minister from seeking to be a faithful minister. The fact that man can be corrupted by money should not prevent us from giving to the poor, especially those who are of the Household of Faith.

Accountability and an emphasis on local authority can provide the safeguards that are necessary to prevent Indigenous Outreach from becoming a colonial style ministry and ultimately weakening the local congregations that are being served.

In his sixties Workeneh was the oldest missionary supported through Indigenous Outreach. He had become a minister later in life and his authorities felt he was too old to serve as a church planter. They busied Workeneh with visiting the sick and elderly. Workeneh had a passion to start a new church in a new village just outside of Addis Abeba. In desperation he approached me for permission to change churches. I counseled Workeneh to go to his leaders and ask them to send him with their blessing to another congregation. He was overjoyed when he was sent to Birayu where he would be instrumental in the founding of a new congregation that reached over 200 members in about one year.

Local authorities had been respected, Workeneh was sent out with a blessing and the church grew in depth and breadth.

Sixty dollars a month is only just enough for an indigenous minister in Ethiopia to pay his rent and purchase some food. The ministers, especially those with children, still have needs beyond the tiny sum they receive from Indigenous Outreach.

Matteous has a large family, and for years they had struggled to make ends meet as pagan neighbors heckled their faith. One night Matteous' wife began to hemorrhage; she was having a miscarriage in the second trimester of pregnancy. It was a death sentence in rural Ethiopia where access to medicine is limited and transportation only operates in daylight hours.

Through the night Matteous cried out to God in Jesus' name. His simple mud home could not contain his cries for help. Some neighbors pitied; others mocked. "Why doesn't his God hear? Maybe he should cry louder."

At daybreak Matteous carried his wife to the main road where they obtained transport to a government hospital. She was weak and lethargic. The believers in the area began to prepare for a funeral.

On the third day Matteous and his wife, very much alive, walked back to the village. Some of those who had mocked him began to cry out, "Praise the God of Matteous. Praise the God who hears!"

Today Matteous and his family live in a home that they were able to build from the support they receive each month through Indigenous Outreach. The congregation continues to grow and Matteous lives as an example of God's great love and mercy.

Caleb has cerebral palsy. He walks with a limp and his speech is slurred. In Ethiopia many would say that Caleb was cursed, or his parents must have sinned for him to be in such a pathetic state. Yet, Caleb loved Jesus and would tell anyone who would listen of the love that God has for those who believe in Jesus.

Caleb began receiving support through Indigenous Outreach and his authorities sent him to help a struggling congregation. To all their surprise the congregation quickly outgrew the sending church.

"I was amazed that God would call me, a cripple, to serve Him," Caleb said. "It was even more amazing when my brothers and sisters in America started supporting me. People I had never met loved me."

Abebe, which means "flowering", joined the military at age 15. Ethiopia was at war in those days and adventure was to be found in the paratroopers. The adventure came to an end when he landed in a mine field which claimed his right eye and left foot.

In a military hospital he became addicted to pain killers and contemplated suicide. However, a young Christian nurse began to show Abebe the love of Christ.

"The more she loved me the more I hated

her," he said. Still she encouraged Abebe to be thankful for his life. The more he hated her the more love she showed him. Abebe had grown up in an Orthodox family, but he had been rebuked when he questioned the traditions of the church and a passage he had read in Luke 11. Eventually Abebe asked the nurse to tell him more about her faith.

"As she spoke the Gospel I could feel the words sinking into my soul," he said. "I asked her what I could do to be saved, and she said, 'Believe!' I did!" She led him through a prayer of repentance and faith, and encouraged him to seek fellowship in a local church. That night Abebe slept through the night and he never took another pain pill. The next morning Abebe received a small New Testament from the nurse.

When the communists took over, Abebe was sent for indoctrination and told that he could no longer be a Christian. He could not deny his Savior, and he suffered persecution like so many other evangelicals under the reign of the communist Durge.

Abebe was eventually discharged from the military and the communist government collapsed. Without a pension or employment he finished his education and was eventually appointed as an evangelist.

Today Abebe receives a regular stipend from Indigenous Outreach. He continues to walk with a limp and he sees with one eye, but he boldly shares the Gospel as a soldier in the army of the Lord.

As one of only a handful of women supported through Indigenous Outreach, Shemsiya fulfills a role that no man could fill. In Muslim society it is not acceptable for men to speak privately with women. As a former Muslim Shemsiya has gained inroads to entire families as she ministers to women.

Rejected by her family and ridiculed by former friends, Shemsiya has found a new family in the Body of Christ, and she has given praise to God as He has provided for her physical needs through that same family.

Balwa's husband had died years earlier, and she had no children to care for her. As the oldest and possibly poorest member of the rural evangelical congregation, she gave what she could in support of the small persecuted church.

When a windstorm destroyed her small hut, Balwa's Orthodox neighbors added insult to injury. "This is what you get for following the foreign god!"

Getu was moved with compassion, but with an income of only $50 per month he could do little to help Balwa. He approached the leadership of Indigenous Outreach and asked for funds to help rebuild this widow's home.

At the end of the meeting Getu was given enough money to build a home for Balwa and to provide for her food for three months. Then he was handed an additional 10% so that Balwa could give a tithe. The total gift was about $200.

Twenty dollars was near the average monthly income for rural Ethiopians. With tears in his eyes Getu said, "That will be the largest single tithe anyone in the congregation has given."

Only a few years ago Chaka had never heard the Gospel. He had grown up in a rural village in the Oromo region of Ethiopia. His religion was the same as his tribal ancestors who worshiped spirits and followed superstitions.

Chaka's father was a respected witchdoctor who had performed miracles with the aid of demonic spirits. Chaka knew that this power was evil, and when his own daughter became deathly ill he refused to allow his father to perform his magic.

A neighbor told Chaka about a group of Christians in a neighboring village. "They worship the one true and holy God, and He can heal your daughter."

After walking for an hour Chaka arrived at the village where Christians were said to live. He asked them about their God and they told him the Gospel. "I immediately believed and rejoiced," he said. Then they told him that he could pray in the name of Jesus for his daughter, but he had never prayed and they had to teach him.

Chaka returned home, placed his hand on his daughter and prayed, "Dear God, please heal my daughter. In Jesus name, Amen." She was instantly healed.

News quickly spread throughout the village and his whole family was converted to faith in Jesus. Soon over a dozen of Chaka's neighbors were professing Christians. Today there are hundreds in the area who have converted from the worship of spirits to Spirit filled worship of Christ.

Born in 1941 Wondimu grew up in a family that was charmed by the occult and left in ignorance by the rural Orthodox church. When his uncle became a believer and repented of sorcery Wondimu cried out for Jesus to save him too. The response of his family was swift and harsh as they expelled him from home. The local evangelical church took Wondimu in and cared for him. A few years later he became an evangelist and church planter.

Now an elderly man he has helped to start over 30 churches and mentored countless young ministers. To many he is lovingly called "Ababa" which means "Dad."

Ababa is a man that few in the West have ever heard of, yet he is a man of deep faith and commitment. For years he traveled the countryside with only a small poncho type garment called a "gobi" to provide warmth through cold nights.

Now, with regular support for his family and packing a modern insulated sleeping bag, Ababa still travels the countryside and mountains of Ethiopia preaching and teaching the Word of God.

Emmebet was an orphan before she ever knew her parents. Her mother died of tuberculosis and her father abandoned the family. Living with her grandmother and great-grandmother Emmabet struggled to help ends meet by selling grain on the street. Without hope she would soon be selling herself and following in the path of so many street children who contract disease and die a horrid death.

Getachew identified Emmabet as a candidate for support through one of the childcare projects supported by Indigenous Outreach. Soon she was in school, attending tutoring sessions, wearing clean clothes, receiving medical care and eating a hot meal daily. Her grandmother received assistance to begin a small business, and the entire extended family slowly began the process of digging out of poverty.

Today Emmabet is in pharmacy school and will soon graduate to a future that is nothing like her early childhood.

Her life and the entire extended family was changed over seven years for a little over $1,600 that was given $20 per month by her sponsor.

Years after the founding of Indigenous Outreach, I met with the minister who had asked me three times what I wanted in return for his monthly support.

"You said that you just wanted to obey God and love us. I believe you now."

Chapter Ten
Two Questions

I have often heard the statement, "It isn't what you know; it's who you know."

In many congregations of Christians today it seems that we know an awful lot about God. We have the Bible in many editions and languages. We have the traditions of two millennia, and a vast array of denominations. There is charisma and liturgy, variety of styles and exciting programs in multi-million dollar buildings. There are satellites that circle the globe broadcasting various streams of teaching and preaching. Words fill the air.

Yet many have reduced the Gospel to a message of cheap grace. "God loves you. Jesus died for you. Just ask Him into your heart and He will make all things new." It is as though Jesus' crucifixion is a fact that must be believed with no repentance or response on our part beyond "receiving Jesus." It is as though God is asking us for a simple favor that we might make room in our hearts for Jesus so that He might fill that "God-sized hole."

Jesus was never once recorded to say, "Ask me into your heart." Rather He commanded that we "believe and repent" and that we take up our crosses and follow Him.

We have failed to remember that the Resurrection followed Jesus' death and that our suffering Savior is also the glorified God of the Universe. He demands our obedience!

We will all come to the end of the journey one day, and two questions weigh heavy in importance.

Who is Jesus?

Who are you?

I believe that God is holy, holy, holy. I am also convinced that God's motivation for sending Jesus is that He loves us. For God so loved the world that He gave His only Son that whosoever believes in Him will not perish, but have everlasting life. The faith that saves is a gift from God that we cannot earn. According to His holy scriptures, He chose us; we did not choose Him. Before the foundations of the world His great love motivated the creation of the universe. Great works of love were established before the seas were divided from the dry land. Jesus was not a creation of God to fix our little sin problem. Jesus is God incarnate. He is from everlasting, and His great plan is one of holiness and love.

Do you know this Jesus? Do you know that He is King of Kings and Lord of Lords? Do you know that He is the Prince of Peace? Do you know that He is the Everlasting Father? Do you know Him as the resurrected Lord and Savior?

Who is Jesus? Jesus is Lord and Savior.

Who are you? If you have faith in His gospel you are a child of God, and He created good works for you to be involved in. As His beloved, what are you going to do about it? What is required of you?

I am convinced that many who doubt their salvation are simply being disobedient. Our faith is shaken because we are committing sin, or we refuse to do the will of God.

Love God and love your neighbor as yourself. Believe on His Son and obey. Take up your cross and follow Jesus!

In *Cost of Discipleship* Dietrich Bonheoffer put it this way, "Only those who believe can obey, and only those who obey can believe."

There is no salvation by works, but there is no salvation without works of love. "For as the body without the spirit is dead, so faith without works is dead." (James 2:26) If we say we love God, but we do not love our brother who is in need we are liars and the truth is not in us. (I John 3:16-24).

There are many in need today, and at the moment we have the provision that they need. I do not have a vision to save the world. I know that the needs can be overwhelming, but I also know some dear fellow believers who are in great need. I know children who need to be rescued from the street. I know widows who sleep sitting up because their roofs leak so badly there is not enough dry ground to lie on.

We can no longer look the other way while we indulge our flesh in religiosity and the things of this world. We are required to love in deed and truth. The fast that God demands is that we "share our bread with the hungry." And true religion is that we "care for widows and orphans in their time of need."

The Church in the West is rich, and we often look very much like the Church in Laodicea. However, there is a hopeful message to the Laodiceans, "Behold, I stand at the door and knock. If anyone hears my voice and opens the door, I will come in to him and dine with him, and he with me." This is not a message of evangelism delivered to an unbelieving mass; it is the message of our Lord to His wealthy, indifferent, lukewarm Church.

Now is the time of need, and today is the day of salvation. If you hear His voice, do not harden your heart. Conformity to the image of Christ is not a prayer for a moment; rather, it is a lifetime of faith and obedience that happens slowly by slowly.

For more information about the ministry of
Indigenous Outreach International
visit us on the web at
www.ioiusa.org
www.ioiuk.org

Join us in Ministry

The simplest way to love for God is to
love others in tangible ways.

You can show this kind of love today by supporting
an at-risk for **as little as $20 per month**, or an
entire missionary family for only **$60 per month.
100% of your gift goes directly to the mission
field with no administrative costs taken out.**

Your additional gift of $5 per month helps to
cover our administrative cost.

Your undesignated gift of $100 per month
could be multiplied in the developing world, and
provide for a great variety of urgent needs.

Join us in ministry today by
mailing your check with designation memo to

Indigenous Outreach International
PO Box 10173
Jackson, TN 38308-0102

Or to begin automatic monthly contributions
Complete and mail the forms on the following
pages, and send it along with your voided check.

*IOI is recognized by the Internal Revenue Service
as a 501(c)(3) tax-exempt organization.
Your donation is tax-deductible.*

An overview of the ministry

Indigenous Outreach International
Established for the purpose of making disciples for Christ.

Missionary Support
Our Primary ministry is the financial, educational, technical and prayer support of indigenous ministers and churches.

Child Sponsorship
IOI has partnered with indigenous programs to provide basic care for at risk children.

Human Needs
The Micah Fund helps provide for physical and educational needs of the poor.

Community Development
Funding for community development projects such as church buildings, housing, clean water and sanitation.

Bibles and Literature
Bibles and Christian literature are provided to ministers free of charge.

Sanctuary Village
A campus to be located in rural Ethiopia promoting discipleship through daily prayer, meditation on Scripture, formal study, vocational training and the ministries of hospitality and mercy.

How you can be involved

Name:_____
Address: _____
City: _____ State:___ Zip:_____
Country: _____ Email:_____
Denominational Preference (if any) _____

I am interested in (tick all that apply):
    ___ supporting an indigenous missionary
    ___ supporting an at-risk child
    ___ Volunteering   ___ Ethiopia
    ___ Internship   ___ Brazil
    ___ Mission Team   ___ Europe
___ I would like to start my support immediately
    and mail my support monthly/annually:
    ___ an indigenous minister ($65 per month)
    ___ an at-risk child ($25 per month)
    ___ the ministry of IOI $_____ per month
___ This is a one time gift for;
    ___ $_____ where needed most
    ___ $_____ for _____
___ Add me to the Newsletter mailing list
___ Send me a copy of *Slowly by Slowly* to share
    with a friend ($10 suggested donation).
___ Please send weekly prayer alerts by email.

Please attach your check and mail with this form to:

I.O.I.
PO Box 10173
Jackson, Tennessee 38308

Or to begin automatic monthly contributions complete and mail the form on the following page, and send it along with your voided check

Direct Debit Form

By submitting the completed form along with your voided check, you are giving permission for IOI to make withdrawals from your account. We will debit your account on the 5th day of every month. This will continue until you send us a written notice of cancellation (please allow six weeks). Also, please do notify us if you close your account.

I (we) hereby authorize Indigenous Outreach International, Inc. to initiate entries to my (our) checking/savings account at the financial institution named on the attached voided check. This authority will remain until I (we) notify Indigenous Outreach in writing to cancel it in such time to afford Indigenous Outreach and the financial institute a reasonable opportunity to act upon it. He amount listed below will be debited from my account on the 5th day of every month or on the next business day thereafter.

Name on the Account:_____
Donation to be debited from:
Checking __ Savings __

Amount authorized to be debited:
____ $25 monthly to support one child
____ $65 monthly to support one missionary
____ $100 monthly to support I.O.I.
____ $_____ Monthly for _____
Signature:_____ Date:_____

Please attach your voided check and mail with this form to:
I.O.I.
PO Box 10173, Jackson, Tennessee 38308

LaVergne, TN USA
29 August 2009
156362LV00004B/2/P